FAVORITE
BrandName
RECIPES™

Dump Dinners

Simple and sensational one-dish recipes

Publications International, Ltd.

Pictured on the front cover: Skillet Pasta Roma *(page 20)*.

Pictured on the back cover *(left to right):* Mexican Casserole with Tortilla Chips *(page 18)* and Bow Tie Pasta Bowl *(page 76)*.

ISBN: 978-1-4508-9343-5

Library of Congress Control Number: 2014944048

Manufactured in China.

8 7 6 5 4 3 2 1

Microwave Cooking: Microwave ovens vary in wattage. Use the cooking times as guidelines and check for doneness before adding more time.

Preparation/Cooking Times: Preparation times are based on the approximate amount of time required to assemble the recipe before cooking, baking, chilling or serving. These times include preparation steps such as measuring, chopping and mixing. The fact that some preparations and cooking can be done simultaneously is taken into account. Preparation of optional ingredients and serving suggestions is not included.

Publications International, Ltd.

CONTENTS

DELICIOUSLY
Simple Skillets

Swirly Noodle Taco Skillet

- 1 pound ground beef
- 1 onion, diced (about 1 cup)
- 1 packet (1.25 ounces) ORTEGA® Taco Seasoning Mix
- 1 can (7 ounces) ORTEGA® Fire-Roasted Diced Green Chilies
- 1 jar (16 ounces) ORTEGA® Salsa, any variety
- ½ pound rotini or fusilli pasta, uncooked

    Shredded Cheddar cheese (optional)

BROWN ground beef and onion in large skillet over medium-high heat 6 to 8 minutes, stirring to break up meat. Drain fat.

ADD taco seasoning mix, chilies, salsa and 2 cups water; stir to combine. Add pasta and stir. Reduce heat to low. Cover and cook 12 to 14 minutes or until pasta is cooked through. Serve with cheese.

Makes 6 servings

TIP: This dish also makes a great taco filling for ORTEGA® Yellow Corn Taco Shells or soft flour tortillas.

PREP TIME: 5 minutes
START TO FINISH TIME: 25 minutes

Chicken Couscous

- 1 tablespoon olive oil
- 8 ounces boneless skinless chicken breasts, cut into 1-inch cubes
- 4 medium zucchini, sliced
- 1 can (about 14 ounces) diced tomatoes
- 1 can (about 14 ounces) reduced-sodium chicken broth
- 1 teaspoon dried Italian seasoning
- 1 cup uncooked whole wheat couscous

1. Heat oil in large skillet over medium-high heat. Add chicken; cook and stir 4 minutes or until lightly browned.

2. Add zucchini, tomatoes, broth and Italian seasoning; simmer over low heat 15 minutes, stirring occasionally.

3. Remove from heat. Stir in couscous; cover and let stand 7 minutes. Fluff with fork.

Makes 4 servings

SPANISH RICE WITH CHORIZO

4 links Spanish-style chorizo sausage (about 12 ounces), diagonally sliced

1 green bell pepper, diced

1½ cups uncooked instant rice

1 can (about 14 ounces) diced tomatoes with garlic and onions

1 cup chicken broth or water

2 green onions, chopped

Salt and black pepper

1. Cook and stir sausage and bell pepper in large nonstick skillet over medium heat 5 minutes or until bell pepper is tender.

2. Stir in rice, tomatoes, broth and green onions; bring to a boil over high heat. Reduce heat to medium-low; cover and simmer 8 to 10 minutes or until liquid is absorbed and rice is tender. Season with salt and black pepper.

Makes 4 servings

TIP: For a vegetarian version, substitute soy-based sausages for the chorizo and add 1 tablespoon vegetable oil to the skillet with the sausages and bell pepper. Substitute vegetable broth or water for the chicken broth.

Easy Skillet Ravioli

  1 **package (about 24 ounces) frozen cheese ravioli**

2¼ **cups water**

  ½ **teaspoon salt**

  1 **jar (1 pound 8 ounces) RAGÚ® Chunky Pasta Sauce**

  ¼ **cup heavy cream, half-and-half, evaporated milk, milk or nondairy creamer (optional)**

1. In 12-inch nonstick skillet, bring ravioli, water and salt to a boil over high heat. Continue boiling, stirring gently to separate ravioli, 5 minutes.

2. Stir in Pasta Sauce. Cook, covered, over medium heat 10 minutes or until ravioli are tender, stirring occasionally. Stir in cream and heat through. Garnish, if desired, with grated Parmesan cheese.

Makes 4 servings

PREP TIME: 5 minutes
COOK TIME: 20 minutes

Southwestern Turkey Stew

1 tablespoon vegetable oil

1 small onion, finely chopped

1 clove garlic, minced

2 cups reduced-sodium chicken broth

2 cups smoked turkey breast, cut into ½-inch pieces

2 cups frozen corn

1 can (about 14 ounces) diced tomatoes

1 package (about 8 ounces) red beans and rice mix

1 to 2 canned chipotle peppers in adobo sauce, drained and minced

Chopped green onion (optional)

1. Heat oil in large skillet over medium-high heat. Add onion and garlic; cook and stir 3 minutes or until onion is translucent.

2. Add broth; bring to a boil. Stir in turkey, corn, tomatoes, rice mix and chipotle pepper. Reduce heat to low; cover and cook about 20 minutes or until rice is tender. Let stand 3 minutes. Sprinkle with green onion, if desired.

Makes 4 servings

PICADILLO TACOS

      6 ounces ground beef

      ½ cup chopped green bell pepper

      ½ teaspoon ground cumin

      ½ teaspoon chili powder

      ⅛ teaspoon ground cinnamon

      ½ cup chunky salsa

      1 tablespoon golden raisins

      4 (6-inch) corn tortillas, warmed

         Toppings: shredded lettuce, shredded Cheddar cheese and chopped tomato

1. Combine ground beef, bell pepper, cumin, chili powder and cinnamon in large nonstick skillet; cook and stir over medium heat until beef is browned.

2. Stir in salsa and raisins; simmer over low heat 5 minutes or until beef is cooked through, stirring occasionally.

3. Divide meat mixture evenly among tortillas; serve with desired toppings.

Makes 2 servings

SKILLET PESTO TORTELLINI

1¼ cups water

1¼ cups milk

1 package (about 1 ounce) creamy pesto sauce mix

1 package (16 ounces) frozen vegetable medley

1 package (12 ounces) frozen tortellini

Dash ground red pepper

½ cup (2 ounces) shredded mozzarella cheese

1. Combine water, milk and sauce mix in large deep skillet; bring to a boil over high heat.

2. Stir in vegetables, tortellini and ground red pepper; return to a boil. Reduce heat to medium-high; cook 8 to 10 minutes or until pasta is tender and sauce has thickened, stirring occasionally. Sprinkle with mozzarella.

Makes 4 servings

SPICY CHICKEN CHILI MAC

 1 can (about 14½ ounces) whole peeled tomatoes, cut up

2½ cups water

 1 cup PACE® Picante Sauce

 1 tablespoon chili powder

 ¼ teaspoon garlic powder **or** 2 cloves garlic, minced

 ¼ teaspoon salt

 ¾ cup uncooked elbow macaroni

 2 cups cubed cooked chicken or turkey

1. Mix tomatoes, water, picante sauce, chili powder, garlic and salt in a 10-inch skillet over medium-high heat. Heat to a boil. Stir in the macaroni. Cover and cook over low heat for 15 minutes or until macaroni is done, stirring often.

2. Add the chicken and heat through. Garnish with shredded cheese and sour cream, if desired.

Makes 4 servings

TOTAL TIME: 25 minutes

MEXICAN CASSEROLE WITH TORTILLA CHIPS

- 2 teaspoons olive oil
- 12 ounces ground turkey
- 1 can (about 14 ounces) stewed tomatoes
- ½ (16-ounce) package frozen bell pepper stir-fry blend, thawed
- ¾ teaspoon ground cumin
- ½ teaspoon salt
- ½ cup (2 ounces) finely shredded sharp Cheddar cheese
- 2 ounces tortilla chips, crushed

1. Heat oil in large skillet over medium heat. Add turkey; cook until no longer pink, stirring to break up meat.

2. Stir in tomatoes, bell peppers, cumin and salt; bring to a boil. Reduce heat to low; cover and simmer 20 minutes or until vegetables are tender. Sprinkle with Cheddar cheese and chips.

Makes 4 servings

VARIATION: Sprinkle chips into a casserole. Spread cooked turkey mixture evenly over the chips and top with cheese.

Skillet Pasta Roma

½ pound Italian sausage, sliced or crumbled

1 large onion, coarsely chopped

1 large clove garlic, minced

2 cans (14.5 ounces each) DEL MONTE® Diced Tomatoes with Basil, Garlic & Oregano

1 can (8 ounces) DEL MONTE® Tomato Sauce

1 cup water

8 ounces uncooked rotini or other spiral pasta

8 mushrooms, sliced (optional)

Grated Parmesan cheese and fresh parsley sprigs (optional)

1. Brown sausage in large skillet. Add onion and garlic. Cook until onion is soft; drain. Stir in undrained tomatoes, tomato sauce, water and pasta.

2. Cover and bring to a boil; reduce heat. Simmer, covered, 25 to 30 minutes or until pasta is tender, stirring occasionally.

3. Stir in mushrooms, if desired; simmer 5 minutes. Serve in skillet garnished with cheese and parsley, if desired.

Makes 4 servings

Sweet and Sour Beef

1 pound ground beef

1 small onion, thinly sliced

2 teaspoons minced fresh ginger

1 package (16 ounces) frozen Asian-style vegetables

6 to 8 tablespoons bottled sweet and sour sauce
   or sauce from vegetable mix

Hot cooked rice

1. Cook beef, onion and ginger in large skillet over medium-high heat 6 to 8 minutes or until beef is browned, stirring to break up meat. Drain fat.

2. Stir in vegetables and sauce; cover and cook 6 to 8 minutes or until vegetables are heated through, stirring occasionally. Serve over rice.

Makes 4 servings

SKILLET SOUTHWEST CHILI

- 1 pound lean ground beef
- 2 cans (14.5 ounces each) DEL MONTE® Diced Tomatoes with Onion and Garlic
- 1 can (15 ounces) low-sodium black or kidney beans, rinsed and drained
- 1 can (4 ounces) diced green chiles
- 1 tablespoon chili powder

   Green onions or cilantro (optional)

1. Brown beef in large skillet; drain.

2. Add undrained tomatoes, beans, chiles and chili powder; simmer 10 minutes, stirring occasionally. Garnish with green onions, if desired.

Makes 4 servings

PREP TIME: 10 minutes
COOK TIME: 20 minutes
TOTAL TIME: 30 minutes

Mushroom and Chicken Skillet

- 1 pound boneless skinless chicken breasts, cut into bite-size pieces
- 1 can (about 14 ounces) chicken broth
- ¼ cup water
- 2 cups uncooked instant rice
- ½ teaspoon dried thyme
- 8 ounces mushrooms, thinly sliced
- 1 can (10¾ ounces) cream of celery soup, undiluted
  Chopped fresh parsley

1. Combine chicken, broth and water in large skillet; bring to a boil over medium-high heat. Stir in rice and thyme; top with mushrooms. (Do not stir mushrooms into rice.) Cover skillet; turn off heat and let stand 5 minutes.

2. Gently stir in soup; cook over low heat 5 minutes or until heated through. Sprinkle with parsley.

Makes 4 servings

Asian Beef and Vegetables

- 1 pound ground beef or turkey
- 1 large onion, coarsely chopped
- 2½ cups (8 ounces) frozen mixed vegetable medley, such as carrots, broccoli and red peppers, thawed
- 2 cloves garlic, minced
- ½ cup stir-fry sauce
- 1 can (3 ounces) chow mein noodles

1. Brown beef and onion in large skillet over medium-high heat 6 to 8 minutes, stirring to break up meat. Drain fat.

2. Add vegetables and garlic; cook and stir 2 minutes or until heated through.

3. Stir in stir-fry sauce; cook 30 seconds or until hot. Serve over chow mein noodles.

Makes 4 servings

Quick Skillet Chicken & Macaroni Parmesan

1 jar (24 ounces) PREGO® Traditional Italian Sauce or Tomato, Basil & Garlic Italian Sauce

¼ cup grated Parmesan cheese

1 can (12.5 ounces) SWANSON® Premium White Chunk Chicken Breast in Water, drained

2 cups elbow pasta, cooked and drained (about 3 cups)

1 cup shredded mozzarella cheese (about 4 ounces)

1. Heat the Italian sauce, Parmesan cheese, chicken and pasta in a 10-inch skillet over medium-high heat to a boil. Reduce the heat to medium and cook for 10 minutes or until the mixture is hot and bubbling, stirring occasionally.

2. Sprinkle with the mozzarella cheese. Let stand for 5 minutes or until the cheese is melted.

Makes 4 servings

KITCHEN TIP: You may substitute 3 cans (4.5 ounces **each**) Swanson® Premium White Chunk Chicken Breast in Water, drained, for the 12.5-ounce can.

PREP TIME: 15 minutes
COOK TIME: 15 minutes
STAND TIME: 5 minutes

ALL-IN-ONE BURGER STEW

- 1 **pound ground beef**
- 2 **cups frozen Italian-style vegetables**
- 1 **can (about 14 ounces) diced tomatoes with basil and garlic**
- 1 **can (about 14 ounces) beef broth**
- 2½ **cups uncooked medium egg noodles**
  - **Salt and black pepper**

1. Brown beef in large skillet over medium-high heat 6 to 8 minutes, stirring to break up meat. Drain fat.

2. Stir in vegetables, tomatoes and broth; bring to a boil over high heat.

3. Add noodles; cover and cook over medium heat 12 to 15 minutes or until vegetables and noodles are tender. Season with salt and pepper.

Makes 6 servings

QUICK-FIX
CASSEROLES

HAM ASPARAGUS GRATIN

1 can (10¾ ounces) CAMPBELL'S® Condensed Cream
   of Asparagus Soup

½ cup milk

¼ teaspoon onion powder

¼ teaspoon ground black pepper

1½ cups cooked cut asparagus

1½ cups cubed cooked ham

2¼ cups corkscrew-shaped pasta (rotini), cooked
   and drained

1 cup shredded Cheddar cheese or Swiss cheese
   (about 4 ounces)

1. Stir the soup, milk, onion powder, black pepper, asparagus, ham, pasta and ½ cup cheese in a 2-quart shallow baking dish.

2. Bake at 400°F. for 25 minutes or until the ham mixture is hot and bubbling. Stir the ham mixture. Sprinkle with the remaining cheese.

3. Bake for 5 minutes or until the cheese is melted.

Makes 4 servings

Shrimp and Chicken Paella

- ¾ cup cooked rice
- 2 cans (about 14 ounces each) diced tomatoes, divided
- ½ teaspoon ground turmeric *or* ⅛ teaspoon saffron threads
- 12 ounces medium raw shrimp, peeled and deveined (with tails on)
- 2 chicken tenders (about 4 ounces), cut into 1-inch pieces
- 1 cup frozen peas

1. Preheat oven to 400°F. Spray 8-inch square baking dish with nonstick cooking spray. Spread rice in prepared dish.

2. Pour one can of tomatoes over rice; sprinkle with turmeric. Arrange shrimp and chicken over tomatoes; top with peas. Drain remaining can of tomatoes, discarding juice. Spread tomatoes evenly over shrimp and chicken.

3. Cover and bake 30 minutes. Let stand, covered, 5 minutes before serving.

Makes 4 servings

Hearty Potato and Sausage Bake

- 1 pound new red potatoes, cut into halves or quarters
- 1 onion, sliced
- 8 ounces baby carrots
- 2 tablespoons butter, melted
- 1 teaspoon salt
- 1 teaspoon garlic powder
- ½ teaspoon dried thyme
- ½ teaspoon black pepper
- 1 pound cooked chicken sausage or turkey sausage, cut into ¼-inch slices

1. Preheat oven to 400°F. Spray 13×9-inch baking dish with nonstick cooking spray.

2. Combine potatoes, onion, carrots, butter, salt, garlic powder, thyme and pepper in prepared baking dish; toss to coat.

3. Bake 30 minutes. Add sausage; mix well. Bake 15 to 20 minutes or until potatoes are tender and golden brown.

Makes 4 to 6 servings

CREAMY TORTELLINI WITH CHICKEN

2 cups PREGO® Fresh Mushroom Italian Sauce

⅓ cup half-and-half

1 package (16 ounces) frozen cheese-filled tortellini, cooked and drained

2 cups cooked chicken strips

1 cup shredded mozzarella cheese (4 ounces)

¼ cup grated Parmesan cheese

1. Stir the Italian sauce and half-and-half in an 11×8-inch (2-quart) shallow baking dish.

2. Add the tortellini, chicken and ½ **cup** of the mozzarella cheese. Stir well to coat. Top with the Parmesan cheese and remaining mozzarella cheese.

3. Bake at 400°F. for 20 minutes or until hot.

Makes 4 servings

EASY SUBSTITUTION TIP: Substitute 1 cup coarsely chopped mushrooms and Prego® Traditional Sauce for the Prego® Fresh Mushroom Italian Sauce.

PREP TIME: 15 minutes
BAKE TIME: 20 minutes

BEEF IN WINE SAUCE

  4 pounds boneless beef chuck roast, cut into
       1½- to 2-inch pieces

  2 cans (10¾ ounces each) condensed golden mushroom
       soup, undiluted

  1 can (8 ounces) sliced mushrooms, drained

  ¾ cup dry sherry

  2 tablespoons garlic powder

  1 package (1 ounce) dry onion soup mix

  1 bag (20 ounces) frozen sliced carrots, thawed

1. Preheat oven to 325°F. Spray 4-quart casserole with nonstick cooking spray.

2. Combine beef, soup, mushrooms, sherry, garlic powder and dry soup mix in prepared casserole; mix well.

3. Cover and bake 3 hours or until beef is tender. Stir in carrots during last 15 minutes of cooking.

Makes 6 to 8 servings

Easy Chicken & Biscuits

- 1 can (10¾ ounces) CAMPBELL'S® Condensed Cream of Broccoli Soup (Regular or 98% Fat Free)
- 1 can (10¾ ounces) CAMPBELL'S® Condensed Cream of Potato Soup
- ⅔ cup milk
- ½ teaspoon poultry seasoning
- ⅛ teaspoon ground black pepper
- 2 cups frozen mixed vegetables
- 2 cups cubed cooked chicken or turkey
- 1 package refrigerated buttermilk biscuits (10 biscuits)

1. Stir the soups, milk, poultry seasoning, black pepper, vegetables and chicken in a 2-quart shallow baking dish.

2. Bake at 400°F. for 20 minutes or until the chicken mixture is hot and bubbling. Cut each biscuit into quarters. Stir the chicken mixture. Top with the biscuits.

3. Bake for 15 minutes or until the biscuits are golden brown.

Makes 4 servings

KITCHEN TIP: Substitute Campbell's® Condensed Cream of Celery Soup for the Cream of Broccoli.

PREP TIME: 10 minutes
BAKE TIME: 35 minutes
TOTAL TIME: 45 minutes

Baked Halibut Casserole

4   fresh or thawed frozen halibut steaks (1 inch thick, about 6 ounces each), rinsed

Salt and black pepper to taste

1   can (8 ounces) tomato sauce

1   package (12 ounces) frozen mixed vegetables such as broccoli, peas, onions and bell peppers

Hot cooked rice (optional)

1. Preheat oven to 350°F. Place halibut in 13×9-inch baking pan; season with salt and pepper.

2. Top fish with tomato sauce and mixed vegetables; season with salt and pepper.

3. Bake 25 to 30 minutes or until fish just begins to flake when tested with fork. Serve over rice, if desired.

Makes 4 servings

E-Z Chicken Tortilla Bake

1 can (10¾ ounces) condensed tomato soup, undiluted

1 cup ORTEGA® Thick & Chunky Salsa

½ cup milk

2 cups cubed cooked chicken

8 (8-inch) ORTEGA® Flour Soft Tortillas, cut into 1-inch pieces

1 cup (4 ounces) shredded Cheddar cheese, divided

PREHEAT the oven to 400°F. Mix soup, salsa, milk, chicken, tortillas and ½ cup cheese in 2-quart shallow baking dish. Cover; bake 30 minutes or until hot. Top with remaining ½ cup cheese.

Makes 4 servings

TIP: Use turkey instead of chicken for an E-Z Turkey Tortilla Bake.

TIP: Two whole chicken breasts (about 10 ounces each) will yield about 2 cups of chopped cooked chicken.

PREP TIME: 10 minutes
START TO FINISH TIME: 40 minutes

CREAMY SHRIMP AND VEGETABLE CASSEROLE

1 pound fresh or thawed frozen shrimp, peeled and deveined

1 can (10¾ ounces) condensed cream of celery soup, undiluted

½ cup sliced fresh or thawed frozen asparagus (1-inch pieces)

½ cup sliced mushrooms

¼ cup diced red bell pepper

¼ cup sliced green onions

1 clove garlic, minced

¾ teaspoon dried thyme

¼ teaspoon black pepper

Hot cooked rice or orzo (optional)

1. Preheat oven to 375°F. Spray 2-quart baking dish with nonstick cooking spray.

2. Combine shrimp, soup, asparagus, mushrooms, bell pepper, green onions, garlic, thyme and black pepper in prepared baking dish.

3. Cover and bake 30 minutes. Serve over rice, if desired.

Makes 4 servings

Cheesy Tuna Noodle Casserole

- 1 can (10¾ ounces) CAMPBELL'S® Condensed Cream of Mushroom Soup (Regular or 98% Fat Free)
- ½ cup milk
- 1 cup frozen peas
- 2 cans (about 6 ounces each) tuna, drained and flaked
- 2 cups hot cooked medium egg noodles
- ½ cup shredded Cheddar cheese

1. Stir the soup, milk, peas, tuna and noodles in a 1½-quart casserole.

2. Bake at 400°F. for 20 minutes or until hot. Stir.

3. Sprinkle cheese over the tuna mixture. Bake for 2 minutes more or until the cheese melts.

Makes 4 servings

KITCHEN TIP: Substitute your family's favorite frozen vegetable for the peas.

PREP TIME: 10 minutes
BAKE TIME: 22 minutes

CAROLINA BAKED BEANS & PORK CHOPS

- 2 cans (16 ounces each) pork and beans
- ½ cup chopped onion
- ½ cup chopped green bell pepper
- ¼ cup packed light brown sugar
- ¼ cup FRENCH'S® Classic Yellow® Mustard
- 2 tablespoons FRENCH'S® Worcestershire Sauce
- 1 tablespoon FRANK'S® REDHOT® Original Cayenne Pepper Sauce
- 6 boneless pork chops (1 inch thick)

1. Preheat oven to 400°F. Combine all ingredients *except pork chops* in 3-quart shallow baking dish; mix well. Arrange pork chops on top, turning once to coat with sauce.

2. Bake, uncovered, 30 to 35 minutes or until pork is no longer pink in center. Stir beans around chops once during baking. Serve with green beans or mashed potatoes, if desired.

Makes 6 servings

PREP TIME: 10 minutes
COOK TIME: 30 minutes

CREAMY CHICKEN AND RICE BAKE

- 1 can (12 fluid ounces) NESTLÉ® CARNATION® Evaporated Milk
- 1 package (3 ounces) cream cheese, softened
- 1 can (10¾ ounces) cream of chicken soup
- ½ cup water
- ½ teaspoon garlic powder
- ⅛ teaspoon ground black pepper
- 1 bag (16 ounces) frozen broccoli, cauliflower and carrot mix, thawed
- 2 cups cubed cooked chicken
- 1½ cups uncooked instant white rice
- ½ cup (2 ounces) shredded cheddar cheese

PREHEAT oven to 350°F. Grease 13×9-inch baking dish.

COMBINE evaporated milk and cream cheese in baking dish with wire whisk until smooth. Add soup, water, garlic powder and black pepper; mix well. Add vegetables, chicken and rice. Cover tightly with foil.

BAKE for 35 minutes. Uncover; top with cheese. Bake for an additional 10 to 15 minutes or until cheese is melted and mixture is bubbly. Let stand 5 minutes before serving.

Makes 8 to 10 servings

PREP TIME: 15 minutes
BAKE TIME: 45 minutes

Easy Chicken Chalupas

8 (8-inch) flour tortillas

3 cups shredded cooked chicken (from 1 rotisserie chicken)

2 cups (8 ounces) shredded Cheddar cheese

1 cup mild green salsa

1 cup mild red salsa

1. Preheat oven to 350°F. Spray 13×9-inch baking dish with nonstick cooking spray.

2. Place two tortillas in bottom of prepared baking dish, overlapping slightly. Layer tortillas with ¾ cup chicken, ½ cup cheese and ¼ cup of each salsa. Repeat layers three times.

3. Bake 25 minutes or until bubbly and heated through.

Makes 6 servings

TIP: Serve this easy main dish with toppings such as sour cream, chopped cilantro, sliced black olives, sliced green onions and sliced avocado.

CREAMY 3-CHEESE PASTA

1 can (10¾ ounces) CAMPBELL'S® Condensed Cream of Mushroom Soup (Regular or 98% Fat Free)

1 package (8 ounces) shredded two-cheese blend (about 2 cups)

⅓ cup grated Parmesan cheese

1 cup milk

¼ teaspoon ground black pepper

3 cups corkscrew-shaped pasta (rotini), cooked and drained

1. Stir the soup, cheeses, milk and black pepper in a 1½-quart casserole. Stir in the pasta.

2. Bake at 400°F. for 20 minutes or until the pasta mixture is hot and bubbling.

Makes 4 servings

PREP TIME: 20 minutes
BAKE TIME: 20 minutes
TOTAL TIME: 40 minutes

Quick Beef Stew in Foil

1   sheet (20×12 inches) heavy-duty foil

8   ounces boneless beef top sirloin steak, cut into
    1-inch pieces

1   medium red potato, peeled and cut into ¾-inch cubes

1   cup frozen mixed vegetables

⅔   cup beef gravy

½   teaspoon dried parsley flakes

¼   teaspoon salt

¼   teaspoon dried thyme

⅛   teaspoon black pepper

1. Preheat oven to 450°F. Spray sheet of foil with nonstick cooking spray.

2. Combine steak, potato, vegetables, gravy, parsley flakes, salt, thyme and pepper in medium bowl; mix well. Spoon beef mixture into center of foil sheet. Double fold sides and ends of foil to seal packet, leaving head space for heat circulation. Place packet on baking sheet.

3. Bake 30 minutes or until beef is tender. Carefully open one end of packet to allow steam to escape.

Makes 2 servings

Gumbo Casserole

2 cans (10¾ ounces each) CAMPBELL'S® Condensed Chicken Gumbo Soup

1 soup can water

1 teaspoon dried minced onion

½ teaspoon Cajun seasoning

½ teaspoon garlic powder

1 cup frozen okra, thawed

¾ cup **uncooked** instant white rice

½ pound cooked ham, diced (about 1½ cups)

½ pound cooked shrimp, peeled and deveined

1. Heat the oven to 375°F. Stir the soup, water, onion, Cajun seasoning, garlic powder, okra, rice, ham and shrimp in a 2-quart casserole.

2. Bake for 35 minutes or until the gumbo is hot and bubbling. Stir the gumbo before serving.

Makes 4 servings

KITCHEN TIP: Try stirring in a little diced andouille sausage for even more Cajun-style flavor!

PREP TIME: 15 minutes
COOK TIME: 35 minutes
TOTAL TIME: 50 minutes

HOMESTYLE CHICKEN & RICE CASSEROLE

- 1 cup long grain white rice
- 1 can (14 ounces) chicken broth
- ¾ cup chopped onion
- 2 cups small broccoli florets
- 4 bone-in chicken breast halves (2½ pounds)
- 1 teaspoon paprika
- 1 teaspoon thyme leaves
- 1 teaspoon garlic salt
- 2 cups (8 ounces) SARGENTO® Fancy Shredded Mild Cheddar Cheese

COMBINE rice, broth, onion and broccoli in 11×7-inch baking pan. Place chicken over rice mixture. Combine paprika, thyme and garlic salt in small bowl; sprinkle over chicken.

COVER with foil; bake in preheated 375°F oven 40 minutes. Uncover; bake 15 minutes more or until liquid is absorbed, rice is tender and chicken is cooked through.

SPRINKLE chicken and rice with cheese. Bake 5 minutes more or until cheese is melted.

Makes 4 servings

PREP TIME: 15 minutes
COOK TIME: 60 minutes

ONE-POT
WONDERS

SHRIMP AND PEPPER NOODLE BOWL

- 4 cups water
- 2 packages (3 ounces each) shrimp-flavored ramen noodles
- 8 ounces frozen cooked medium shrimp *or* 1 package (8 ounces) frozen cooked baby shrimp
- 1 cup frozen bell pepper strips
- ¼ cup chopped green onions
- 1 tablespoon soy sauce
- ½ teaspoon hot pepper sauce
- 2 tablespoons chopped fresh cilantro (optional)

1. Bring water to a boil in large saucepan over high heat. Reserve seasoning packets from noodles. Break up noodles; add to boiling water. Add shrimp and bell pepper; cook 3 minutes.

2. Stir in seasoning packets, green onions, soy sauce and hot pepper sauce; cook 1 minute. Sprinkle with cilantro, if desired.

Makes 4 servings

Chicken Florentine in Minutes

  3 cups water

  1 cup milk

  2 tablespoons butter

  2 packages (about 4 ounces each) fettuccine Alfredo
     or stroganoff pasta mix

  ¼ teaspoon black pepper

  1 package (about 10 ounces) refrigerated fully cooked
     chicken breast strips, cut into ½-inch pieces

  4 cups baby spinach, coarsely chopped

  ¼ cup diced roasted red pepper

  ¼ cup sour cream

1. Bring water, milk and butter to a boil in large saucepan over medium-high heat. Stir in pasta mix and black pepper. Reduce heat to medium; cook 8 minutes or until pasta is tender, stirring occasionally.

2. Stir in chicken, spinach and roasted pepper; cook 2 minutes or until heated through. Remove from heat; stir in sour cream.

Makes 4 servings

SIMPLE TURKEY CHILI

1 pound ground turkey

1 small onion, chopped

1 can (about 28 ounces) diced tomatoes

1 can (about 15 ounces) chickpeas, rinsed and drained

1 can (about 15 ounces) kidney beans, rinsed and drained

1 can (about 15 ounces) black beans, rinsed and drained

1 can (6 ounces) tomato sauce

1 can (4 ounces) chopped green chiles

1 to 2 tablespoons chili powder

1. Cook turkey and onion in large saucepan over medium-high heat until turkey is cooked through, stirring to break up turkey. Drain fat.

2. Stir in tomatoes, chickpeas, beans, tomato sauce, chiles and chili powder; bring to a boil over high heat. Reduce heat to medium-low; simmer about 20 minutes, stirring occasionally.

Makes 8 servings

Italian Sausage and Vegetable Stew

1 pound hot or mild Italian sausage links, cut into
   1-inch pieces

1 package (16 ounces) frozen vegetable blend,
   such as onions and bell peppers

2 medium zucchini, sliced

1 can (about 14 ounces) Italian-style diced tomatoes

1 can (4 ounces) sliced mushrooms, drained

4 cloves garlic, minced

1. Brown sausage in large saucepan over medium-high heat
5 minutes, stirring frequently. Drain fat.

2. Add frozen vegetables, zucchini, tomatoes, mushrooms
and garlic; bring to a boil. Reduce heat to medium-low; cover
and simmer 10 minutes. Uncover; cook 5 to 10 minutes or until
thickened slightly.

Makes 6 servings

Tortellini-Vegetable Toss

1 jar (24 ounces) PREGO® Chunky Garden Combination Italian Sauce

1 bag (16 ounces) frozen vegetable combination (broccoli, cauliflower, carrots)

1 package (16 ounces) frozen cheese-filled tortellini, cooked and drained

Grated Parmesan cheese

1. Heat the Italian sauce in a 3-quart saucepan over medium heat to a boil. Stir in the vegetables. Cover and cook for 10 minutes or until the vegetables are tender-crisp, stirring occasionally.

2. Put the tortellini in a large serving bowl. Pour the vegetable mixture over the tortellini. Toss to coat. Serve with the cheese.

Makes 4 servings

PREP TIME: 5 minutes
COOK TIME: 15 minutes
TOTAL TIME: 20 minutes

Spanish Seafood Stew

2 jars (16 ounces each) PACE® Picante Sauce

1 bottle (8 ounces) clam juice

¼ cup dry white wine or water

1 package (3½ ounces) chorizo sausage, sliced

2½ pounds cod, haddock or snapper

24 littleneck clams

Hot cooked regular long-grain white rice

1. Heat picante sauce, clam juice and wine in a 6-quart saucepan over high heat to a boil. **Cover.** Add chorizo, fish and clams.

2. Reduce heat to low and cook for 10 minutes or until done. Serve over rice.

Makes 8 servings

TOTAL TIME: 25 minutes

Bow Tie Pasta Bowl

  3 cups reduced-sodium chicken broth

  6 ounces uncooked bow tie pasta

  ⅛ teaspoon red pepper flakes

1½ cups diced cooked chicken

  1 medium tomato, seeded and diced

  1 cup packed spring greens or spinach, coarsely chopped

  3 tablespoons chopped fresh basil

  ½ teaspoon salt

  1 cup (4 ounces) shredded mozzarella cheese

  2 tablespoons grated Parmesan cheese

1. Bring broth to boil in large saucepan over high heat. Add pasta and red pepper flakes; return to a boil. Reduce heat to medium-low; cover and simmer 10 minutes or until pasta is tender.

2. Add chicken; cook 1 minute. Remove from heat; stir in tomato, greens, basil and salt. Top with mozzarella and Parmesan.

Makes 4 servings

CHILI Á LA MEXICO

- 2 pounds ground beef
- 2 cups finely chopped onions
- 2 cloves garlic, minced
- 1 can (28 ounces) whole peeled tomatoes, undrained, coarsely chopped
- 1 can (6 ounces) tomato paste
- 1½ to 2 tablespoons chili powder
- 1 teaspoon ground cumin
- ¼ teaspoon salt
- ¼ teaspoon ground red pepper
- ¼ teaspoon ground cloves (optional)
- Lime wedges and cilantro sprigs (optional)

1. Brown beef in large saucepan over medium-high heat 6 to 8 minutes, stirring to separate meat. Drain fat. Add onions and garlic; cook and stir over medium heat 5 minutes or until onions are softened.

2. Stir in tomatoes with juice, tomato paste, chili powder, cumin, salt, red pepper and cloves, if desired; bring to a boil over high heat. Reduce heat to low; cover and simmer 30 minutes, stirring occasionally. Serve with lime wedges and cilantro, if desired.

Makes 6 to 8 servings

CURRIED SHRIMP AND NOODLES

  3 **cups water**

  2 **packages (about 1.6 ounces each) instant curry-flavored rice noodle soup mix**

  1 **package (8 ounces) frozen cooked baby shrimp**

  1 **cup frozen bell pepper strips, cut into 1-inch pieces *or* 1 cup frozen peas**

  ¼ **cup chopped green onions**

  ¼ **teaspoon salt**

  ¼ **teaspoon black pepper**

  1 **to 2 tablespoons fresh lime juice**

1. Bring water to a boil in large saucepan over high heat. Add soup mixes, shrimp, bell pepper, green onions, salt and black pepper; cook 3 to 5 minutes or until noodles are tender, stirring frequently.

2. Stir in lime juice. Serve immediately.

Makes 4 servings

Asian Vegetables and Ham

2 cups reduced-sodium chicken broth

1 package (16 ounces) frozen stir-fry vegetables

1 teaspoon sesame oil

4 ounces thinly sliced ham, cut into ½-inch pieces

2 cups uncooked instant white long grain rice

Soy sauce (optional)

1. Combine broth, vegetables and sesame oil in large saucepan; bring to a boil over high heat.

2. Remove from heat; stir in ham and rice. Cover and let stand 5 minutes. Serve with soy sauce, if desired.

Makes 4 servings

VARIATION: Substitute 12 ounces cooked chicken for the ham.

Pesto Turkey & Pasta

¼ cup milk

1 tablespoon margarine or butter

1 (4.7-ounce) package PASTA RONI® Chicken & Broccoli
   Flavor with Linguine

1 pound boneless, skinless turkey or chicken breasts,
   cut into thin strips

1 medium red or green bell pepper, sliced

½ medium onion, chopped

½ cup prepared pesto sauce

¼ cup pine nuts or chopped walnuts, toasted

   Grated Parmesan cheese (optional)

1. In large saucepan, bring 1½ cups water, milk and margarine to a boil. Stir in pasta and Special Seasonings. Reduce heat to medium. Gently boil 1 minute.

2. Add turkey, bell pepper and onion. Return to a boil. Gently boil 8 to 9 minutes or until pasta is tender and turkey is no longer pink inside, stirring occasionally.

3. Stir in pesto. Let stand 3 to 5 minutes before serving. Sprinkle with nuts and cheese, if desired.

Makes 4 servings

TIP: To make your own pesto, blend 2 cups fresh parsley or basil, 2 cloves garlic and ⅓ cup walnuts in a blender or food processor. Slowly add ½ cup olive oil and ¼ cup Parmesan cheese.

PREP TIME: 10 minutes
COOK TIME: 20 minutes

Sausage Bean Stew

1 pound cooked smoked sausage, cut into ¼-inch slices, halved

1 can (15.5 ounces) JOAN OF ARC® Great Northern Beans, rinsed, drained

1 can (15 ounces) ORTEGA® Black Beans, rinsed, drained

1 can (15 ounces) lima beans, drained

1 can (11 ounces) whole kernel corn, drained

1 can (10 ounces) ORTEGA® Fire-Roasted Diced Green Chiles

1 can (10 ounces) diced tomatoes

½ teaspoon salt

⅛ teaspoon black pepper

Hot cooked rice (optional)

COMBINE all ingredients except rice in large saucepan. Cook over medium heat until heated through. Serve over rice, if desired.

Makes 6 servings

PREP TIME: 10 minutes
START TO FINISH TIME: 20 minutes

Confetti Chicken Chili

    2 teaspoons olive oil

    1 pound ground chicken or turkey

    1 large onion, chopped

  3½ cups reduced-sodium chicken broth

    1 can (about 15 ounces) Great Northern beans, rinsed
       and drained

    2 carrots, chopped

    1 medium green bell pepper, chopped

    2 plum tomatoes, chopped

    1 jalapeño pepper,* finely chopped (optional)

    2 teaspoons chili powder

    ½ teaspoon ground red pepper

*Jalapeño peppers can sting and irritate the skin, so wear rubber
gloves when handling peppers and do not touch your eyes.*

1. Heat oil in large saucepan over medium heat. Add chicken
and onion; cook and stir 5 minutes or until chicken is browned.
Drain fat.

2. Stir in broth, beans, carrots, bell pepper, tomatoes, jalapeño,
if desired, chili powder and red pepper; bring to a boil over high
heat. Reduce heat to low; cover and simmer 15 minutes.

Makes 5 servings

Shrimp Alfredo with Sugar Snap Peas

½ cup milk

3 tablespoons margarine or butter

1 (4.7-ounce) package PASTA RONI® Fettuccine Alfredo

1 (9-ounce) package frozen sugar snap peas, thawed

8 ounces cooked, deveined, peeled medium shrimp

½ teaspoon ground lemon pepper

1. In large saucepan, bring 1¼ cups water, milk, margarine, pasta and Special Seasonings to a boil. Reduce heat to low. Gently boil 4 minutes, stirring occasionally.

2. Stir in snap peas, shrimp and lemon pepper; cook 1 to 2 minutes or until pasta is tender. Let stand 3 minutes before serving.

Makes 4 servings

TIP: If you don't have lemon pepper in your cupboard, try Italian seasoning instead.

PREP TIME: 5 minutes
COOK TIME: 15 minutes

Jerk Turkey Stew

- 1 tablespoon vegetable oil
- 1 small red onion, chopped
- 1 clove garlic, minced
- ½ teaspoon ground ginger
- ¼ teaspoon salt
- ¼ teaspoon black pepper
- ⅛ teaspoon ground red pepper
- ⅛ teaspoon ground allspice
- 1 can (about 28 ounces) diced tomatoes
- 3 cups diced cooked turkey
- 2 cups diced cooked sweet potatoes (½-inch pieces)
- ½ cup turkey broth or gravy
- 1 tablespoon lime juice
- 1 tablespoon minced fresh chives

1. Heat oil in large saucepan over medium heat. Add onion and garlic; cook and stir 5 minutes. Add ginger, salt, black pepper, red pepper and allspice; cook 20 seconds. Stir in tomatoes, turkey, sweet potatoes and broth. Reduce heat to low; simmer 15 minutes.

2. Stir in lime juice; cover and let stand 10 minutes. Sprinkle with chives just before serving.

Makes 4 servings

Chicken Tetrazzini

1 can (10¾ ounces) CAMPBELL'S® Condensed Cream of Mushroom Soup (Regular or 98% Fat Free)

¾ cup water

½ cup grated Parmesan cheese

2 tablespoons chopped fresh parsley **or** 2 teaspoons dried parsley flakes

¼ cup chopped red bell pepper **or** pimientos (optional)

½ package (8 ounces) spaghetti, cooked and drained

2 cans (4.5 ounces each) SWANSON® Premium White Chunk Chicken Breast in Water, drained

1. Heat the soup, water, cheese, parsley, red pepper, if desired, spaghetti and chicken in a 2-quart saucepan over medium heat until the mixture is hot and bubbling.

Makes 4 servings

PREP TIME: 20 minutes
COOK TIME: 5 minutes
TOTAL TIME: 25 minutes

SLOW-COOKER
SUPPERS

SLOW COOKER
SOUTHWESTERN PORK ROAST

2½ pounds boneless pork roast

1 envelope LIPTON® Recipe Secrets® Onion Soup Mix

1 can (14½ ounces) diced tomatoes, undrained

2 cans (4 ounces each) chopped green chilies, undrained

3 tablespoons firmly packed brown sugar

2 teaspoons chili powder

1 teaspoon ground cumin

1. In slow cooker, arrange pork. Combine LIPTON® Recipe Secrets® Onion Soup Mix with remaining ingredients; pour over pork.

2. Cook, covered, on low 8 to 10 hours or on high 4 to 6 hours or until pork is tender. Serve, if desired, with hot cooked noodles or rice.

Makes 8 servings

PREP TIME: 5 minutes
COOK TIME: 4 hours (High)

Easy Italian Chicken

4 boneless skinless chicken breasts
(about 4 ounces each)

8 ounces mushrooms, sliced

1 medium onion, chopped

1 medium green bell pepper, chopped

1 medium zucchini, diced

1 jar (26 ounces) pasta sauce

Hot cooked pasta (optional)

1. Combine chicken, mushrooms, onion, bell pepper, zucchini and pasta sauce in slow cooker.

2. Cover; cook on LOW 6 to 8 hours or until chicken is tender. Serve over pasta, if desired.

Makes 4 servings

THREE-BEAN MOLE CHILI

- 1 can (about 15 ounces) chili beans in spicy sauce
- 1 can (about 15 ounces) pinto beans, rinsed and drained
- 1 can (about 15 ounces) black beans, rinsed and drained
- 1 can (about 14 ounces) Mexican- or chili-style diced tomatoes
- 1 large green bell pepper, diced
- 1 small onion, diced
- ½ cup beef, chicken or vegetable broth
- ¼ cup prepared mole paste*
- 2 teaspoons ground cumin
- 2 teaspoons chili powder
- 2 teaspoons ground coriander (optional)
- 2 teaspoons minced garlic

    Toppings: crushed tortilla chips, chopped cilantro or shredded cheese

Mole paste is available in the Mexican aisle of large supermarkets or in specialty markets.

1. Combine beans, tomatoes, bell pepper, onion, broth, mole paste, cumin, chili powder, coriander, if desired, and garlic in slow cooker.

2. Cover; cook on LOW 5 to 6 hours. Serve with desired toppings.

Makes 4 to 6 servings

Super-Easy Beef Burritos >

1 boneless beef chuck roast (2 to 3 pounds)

1 can (28 ounces) enchilada sauce

4 (8-inch) flour tortillas

Toppings: shredded cheese, sour cream, salsa, shredded lettuce and chopped tomatoes

1. Place roast in slow cooker; cover with enchilada sauce.

2. Cover; cook on LOW 6 to 8 hours or until beef begins to fall apart. Shred beef; serve in tortillas with desired toppings.

Makes 4 servings

Harvest Ham Supper

6 carrots, cut into 2-inch pieces

3 medium sweet potatoes, quartered

1 to 1½ pounds boneless ham

1 cup maple syrup

1. Place carrots and sweet potatoes in bottom of slow cooker. Place ham on top of vegetables. Pour syrup over ham and vegetables.

2. Cover; cook on LOW 6 to 8 hours.

Makes 6 servings

Classic Chicken & Rice

3 cans (10¾ ounces each) condensed cream of chicken soup, undiluted

2 cups uncooked instant rice

1 cup water

1 pound boneless skinless chicken breasts or chicken breast tenders

½ teaspoon salt

¼ teaspoon paprika

¼ teaspoon black pepper

½ cup diced celery

1. Combine soup, rice and water in slow cooker. Add chicken; sprinkle with salt, paprika and pepper. Sprinkle celery over chicken.

2. Cover; cook on LOW 6 to 8 hours or on HIGH 3 to 4 hours.

Makes 4 servings

Slow-Cooked Autumn Brisket

- 1 boneless beef brisket (about 3 pounds)
- 1 small head cabbage (about 1 pound), cut into 8 wedges
- 1 large sweet potato (about ¾ pound), peeled and cut into 1-inch pieces
- 1 large onion, cut into 8 wedges
- 1 medium Granny Smith apple, cored and cut into 8 wedges
- 2 cans (10¾ ounces each) CAMPBELL'S® Condensed Cream of Celery Soup (Regular or 98% Fat Free)
- 1 cup water
- 2 teaspoons caraway seed (optional)

1. Place the brisket in a 6-quart slow cooker. Top with the cabbage, sweet potato, onion and apple. Stir the soup, water and caraway seed, if desired, in a small bowl. Pour the soup mixture over the brisket and vegetable mixture.

2. Cover and cook on LOW for 8 to 9 hours* or until the brisket is fork-tender. Season as desired.

Or on HIGH for 4 to 5 hours.

Makes 8 servings

PREP TIME: 20 minutes
COOK TIME: 8 hours
TOTAL TIME: 8 hours 20 minutes

New World Pork Stew

2 small sweet potatoes (about ¾ pound), peeled and cut into 2-inch pieces

1 package (10 ounces) frozen corn

1 package (9 ounces) frozen cut green beans

1 cup chopped onion

1¼ pounds pork stew meat, cut into 1-inch cubes

1 can (about 14 ounces) diced tomatoes

¼ cup water

1 to 2 tablespoons chili powder

½ teaspoon salt

½ teaspoon ground coriander

1. Place sweet potatoes, corn, green beans and onion in slow cooker. Top with pork. Add tomatoes, water, chili powder, salt and coriander.

2. Cover; cook on LOW 7 to 9 hours.

Makes 6 servings

MEATBALLS IN BURGUNDY SAUCE

60 frozen fully cooked meatballs, partially thawed
    and separated

 3 cups chopped onions

1½ cups water

 1 cup Burgundy or other red wine

¼ cup ketchup

 2 packages (about 1 ounce each) beef gravy mix

 1 tablespoon dried oregano

   Hot cooked egg noodles (optional)

1. Combine meatballs, onions, water, wine, ketchup, gravy mix and oregano in slow cooker.

2. Cover; cook on HIGH 4 to 5 hours. Serve over noodles, if desired.

Makes 6 to 8 servings

Pacific Island Chicken & Rice

2 cans (10½ ounces each) CAMPBELL'S® Condensed Chicken Broth

1 cup water

¼ cup soy sauce

2 cloves garlic, minced

8 skinless, boneless chicken thighs (about 2 pounds), cut into 1½-inch pieces

1 medium green or red pepper, cut into 1½-inch pieces (about 1 cup)

4 green onions, cut into 2-inch pieces (about 1 cup)

1 can (20 ounces) pineapple chunks in juice, undrained

1 cup uncooked regular long-grain white rice

Toasted sliced almonds

1. Stir the broth, water, soy sauce, garlic, chicken, pepper, onions, pineapple with juice and rice in 6-quart slow cooker.

2. Cover and cook on LOW for 7 to 8 hours* or until chicken is cooked through.

3. Sprinkle with the almonds before serving.

Or on HIGH for 4 to 5 hours.

Makes 8 servings

KITCHEN TIP: To toast almonds, arrange almonds in single layer in a shallow baking pan. Bake at 350°F. for 10 minutes or until lightly browned.

PREP TIME: 20 minutes
COOK TIME: 7 hours

CARIBBEAN SWEET POTATO AND BEAN STEW

- 2 medium sweet potatoes (about 1 pound), peeled and cut into 1-inch cubes
- 2 cups frozen cut green beans
- 1 can (about 15 ounces) black beans, rinsed and drained
- 1 can (about 14 ounces) vegetable broth
- 1 small onion, sliced
- 2 teaspoons Caribbean jerk seasoning
- ½ teaspoon dried thyme
- ¼ teaspoon salt
- ¼ teaspoon ground cinnamon
- ⅓ cup slivered almonds, toasted*

  Hot pepper sauce (optional)

To toast almonds, spread in single layer on baking sheet. Bake in preheated 350°F oven 8 to 10 minutes or until golden brown, stirring frequently.

1. Combine sweet potatoes, green beans, black beans, broth, onion, jerk seasoning, thyme, salt and cinnamon in slow cooker.

2. Cover; cook on LOW 5 to 6 hours or until vegetables are tender. Serve with almonds and hot pepper sauce, if desired.

Makes 4 servings

Slow Cooker Sausage and Peppers

  1 **envelope LIPTON® Recipe Secrets® Onion Soup Mix**

  4 **medium green bell peppers, sliced (about 4 cups)**

1½ **pounds sweet Italian sausage links**

  1 **can (8 ounces) tomato sauce**

  ½ **teaspoon dried oregano leaves, crushed**

1. In slow cooker, combine LIPTON® Recipe Secrets® Onion Soup Mix with rest of ingredients.

2. Cook, covered, on low 8 to 10 hours or on high 4 to 6 hours, or until sausage is done. Serve over hot cooked pasta or in hero rolls.

Makes 4 servings

PREP TIME: 15 minutes
COOK TIME: 4 hours (High)

Pork with Mustard and Sauerkraut >

  2 jars (32 ounces each) sauerkraut, rinsed and drained

2½ cups water

  3 tablespoons brown mustard

  1 package (1 ounce) dry onion soup mix

  3 pounds boneless pork loin roast

1. Combine sauerkraut, water, mustard and soup mix in slow cooker; mix well. Top with pork.

2. Cover; cook on LOW 8 hours. Slice pork; serve with sauerkraut.

Makes 6 servings

Mushroom-Beef Stew

  1 pound beef stew meat

  1 can (10¾ ounces) condensed cream of mushroom soup, undiluted

  2 cans (4 ounces each) sliced mushrooms, drained

  1 package (1 ounce) dry onion soup mix

     Hot cooked noodles

1. Combine beef, condensed soup, mushrooms and soup mix in slow cooker.

2. Cover; cook on LOW 8 to 10 hours. Serve over noodles.

Makes 4 servings

Beef Bourguignonne

- 1 can (10¾ ounces) CAMPBELL'S® Condensed Golden Mushroom Soup
- 1 cup Burgundy or other dry red wine
- 2 cloves garlic, minced
- 1 teaspoon dried thyme leaves, crushed
- 2 cups small button mushrooms (about 6 ounces)
- 2 cups fresh or thawed frozen baby carrots
- 1 cup frozen small whole onions, thawed
- 1½ pounds beef top round steak, 1½-inches thick, cut into 1-inch pieces

1. Stir the soup, wine, garlic, thyme, mushrooms, carrots, onions and beef in a 3½-quart slow cooker.

2. Cover and cook on LOW for 8 to 9 hours* or until the beef is fork-tender.

Or on HIGH for 4 to 5 hours.

Makes 6 servings

PREP TIME: 10 minutes
COOK TIME: 8 hours

No-Fuss Macaroni and Cheese

  2 cups (about 8 ounces) uncooked elbow macaroni

  4 ounces pasteurized process cheese product, cubed

  1 cup (4 ounces) shredded Cheddar cheese

  ½ teaspoon salt

  ⅛ teaspoon black pepper

1½ cups milk

1. Combine macaroni, cheeses, salt and pepper in slow cooker. Pour milk over top.

2. Cover; cook on LOW 2 to 3 hours, stirring after 20 to 30 minutes.

Makes 6 to 8 servings

VARIATION: Stir in sliced hot dogs or vegetables near the end of cooking. Cover; cook until heated through.

NOTE: As with all macaroni and cheese dishes, the cheese sauce thickens and begins to dry out as it sits. If it becomes too dry, stir in a little extra milk. Do not cook longer than 4 hours.

Slow Cooker Sloppy Joes

  1 **envelope LIPTON® RECIPE SECRETS® Onion Soup Mix**

1½ **pounds ground beef, browned and drained**

  1 **cup water**

  1 **cup ketchup**

  2 **tablespoons firmly packed brown sugar**

  6 **hamburger buns**

1. In slow cooker, combine LIPTON® Recipe Secrets® Onion Soup Mix with rest of ingredients, except hamburger buns.

2. Cook, covered, on low 4 to 6 hours or on high 2 to 3 hours. Serve on hamburger buns.

Makes 6 servings

Easy Beef Stew

1½ to 2 pounds beef stew meat

4 medium potatoes, cubed

4 carrots, cut into 1½-inch pieces *or* 4 cups baby carrots

1 medium onion, cut into 8 pieces

2 cans (8 ounces each) tomato sauce

1 teaspoon salt

½ teaspoon black pepper

1. Combine beef, potatoes, carrots, onion, tomato sauce, salt and pepper in slow cooker.

2. Cover; cook on LOW 8 to 10 hours or until vegetables are tender.

Makes 6 to 8 servings

ACKNOWLEDGMENTS

**The publisher would like to thank the companies
and organizations listed below for the use of
their recipes and photographs in this publication.**

Campbell Soup Company

Del Monte Foods

The Golden Grain Company®

Nestlé USA

Ortega®, A Division of B&G Foods North America, Inc.

Reckitt Benckiser LLC.

Sargento® Foods Inc.

Unilever

METRIC
CONVERSION CHART

VOLUME MEASUREMENTS (dry)

$\frac{1}{8}$ teaspoon	= 0.5 mL
$\frac{1}{4}$ teaspoon	= 1 mL
$\frac{1}{2}$ teaspoon	= 2 mL
$\frac{3}{4}$ teaspoon	= 4 mL
1 teaspoon	= 5 mL
1 tablespoon	= 15 mL
2 tablespoons	= 30 mL
$\frac{1}{4}$ cup	= 60 mL
$\frac{1}{3}$ cup	= 75 mL
$\frac{1}{2}$ cup	= 125 mL
$\frac{2}{3}$ cup	= 150 mL
$\frac{3}{4}$ cup	= 175 mL
1 cup	= 250 mL
2 cups = 1 pint	= 500 mL
3 cups	= 750 mL
4 cups = 1 quart	= 1 L

VOLUME MEASUREMENTS (fluid)

1 fluid ounce (2 tablespoons) = 30 mL
4 fluid ounces ($\frac{1}{2}$ cup) = 125 mL
8 fluid ounces (1 cup) = 250 mL
12 fluid ounces (1$\frac{1}{2}$ cups) = 375 mL
16 fluid ounces (2 cups) = 500 mL

WEIGHTS (mass)

$\frac{1}{2}$ ounce = 15 g
1 ounce = 30 g
3 ounces = 90 g
4 ounces = 120 g
8 ounces = 225 g
10 ounces = 285 g
12 ounces = 360 g
16 ounces = 1 pound = 450 g

DIMENSIONS

$\frac{1}{16}$ inch = 2 mm
$\frac{1}{8}$ inch = 3 mm
$\frac{1}{4}$ inch = 6 mm
$\frac{1}{2}$ inch = 1.5 cm
$\frac{3}{4}$ inch = 2 cm
1 inch = 2.5 cm

OVEN TEMPERATURES

250°F = 120°C
275°F = 140°C
300°F = 150°C
325°F = 160°C
350°F = 180°C
375°F = 190°C
400°F = 200°C
425°F = 220°C
450°F = 230°C

BAKING PAN SIZES

Utensil	Size in Inches/Quarts	Metric Volume	Size in Centimeters
Baking or Cake Pan (square or rectangular)	8×8×2	2 L	20×20×5
	9×9×2	2.5 L	23×23×5
	12×8×2	3 L	30×20×5
	13×9×2	3.5 L	33×23×5
Loaf Pan	8×4×3	1.5 L	20×10×7
	9×5×3	2 L	23×13×7
Round Layer Cake Pan	8×1½	1.2 L	20×4
	9×1½	1.5 L	23×4
Pie Plate	8×1¼	750 mL	20×3
	9×1¼	1 L	23×3
Baking Dish or Casserole	1 quart	1 L	—
	1½ quarts	1.5 L	—
	2 quarts	2 L	—